92 Hol   3302122
Green, Carl R

Doc Holliday

Outlaws and Lawmen of the Wild West

DOC HOLLIDAY

Carl R. Green
✦ and ✦
William R. Sanford

ENSLOW PUBLISHERS, INC.

44 Fadem Road   P.O. Box 38
Box 699   Aldershot
Springfield, N.J. 07081   Hants GU12 6BP
U.S.A.   U.K.

Library of Congress Cataloging-in-Publication Data

Green, Carl R.
    Doc Holliday / Carl R. Green and William R. Sanford.
       p. cm. — (Outlaws and lawmen of the wild west)
    Includes bibliographical references and index.
    ISBN 0-89490-589-9
       1. Holliday, John Henry, 1851–1887—Juvenile literature.
2. Gamblers—West (U.S.)—Biography—Juvenile literature.
I. Sanford, William R. II. Title. III. Series: Green, Carl R.
Outlaws and lawmen of the wild west.
F594.H74G74 1995
978′.02′092—dc20
[B]   94-24845
                                           CIP

Printed in the United States of America

10 9 8 7 6 5 4 3 2 1

Illustration Credits: Arizona Historical Society, pp. 8, 33; Colorado Historical Society, pp. 14, 22; Denver Public Library, Western History Department, pp. 6, 10, 31, 35, 40; Carl R. Green and William R. Sanford, p. 18; National Archives, pp. 20, 24, 29, 36; National Library of Medicine, Prints and Photographs Collection, p. 15.

Cover Illustration: Michael David Biegel

CONTENTS

AUTHORS' NOTE

This book tells the true story of a gambler and gunman known as Doc Holliday. Doc, who began his career as a frontier dentist, was as well-known a hundred years ago as rock stars are now known. His exploits appeared in newspapers, magazines, and dime novels. In more recent years, Doc has been featured in movies and on television. Some of the stories have been made up, but many are true. To the best of the authors' knowledge, all of the events described in this book really happened.

1

A SHOOTOUT FOR THE AGES

In the Wild West an argument over a card game or a woman often led to gunplay. Outlaws and lawmen alike were either quick—or dead.

A sometime dentist named Doc Holliday took a hand in the best known shootout of all. The place was well named—Tombstone, Arizona. The date was Wednesday, October 26, 1881. Three men died that day in the gunfight at the O.K. Corral.

On one side stood the hotheaded Clanton gang. Pitted against the Clantons were Doc and the three Earp brothers. Virgil was town marshal and Morgan was his deputy. Wyatt was a U.S. Marshal. Even though Doc was a gambler and con man, he and Wyatt were close friends.

Ike Clanton, drunk and boastful, started the trouble. On Tuesday night he told all who would listen that there

Today, Tombstone's O.K. Corral dozes peacefully in the Arizona sun. In 1881, it was the scene of the Wild West's most famous gunfight. The shootout helped create the legends that still surround Doc Holliday, Wyatt Earp, and the other men who fought there.

would soon be some shooting. On Wednesday morning Virgil found him lurking in an alley. The tough lawman pistol-whipped Ike. Then he took him to jail for carrying a gun, which was illegal in Tombstone. Released after paying a $25 fine, Ike met Billy Clanton and Frank and Tom McLaury near the O.K. Corral. Word soon reached the Earps that the Clantons were armed and ready for a fight.[1] The lawmen set off to arrest them.

Doc, leaning on his cane, met the Earps outside Hafford's Saloon. To keep warm on the cool fall day, he wore a long topcoat over his gray suit. Wyatt stared at him and said, "Doc, this is our fight. There's no call for you to mix in."

Doc had made up his mind. "That's a hell of a thing

for you to say to me," he snapped.[2] Virgil figured he might need Doc at his side. He deputized the gambler, took his cane, and handed him a shotgun. Doc hid the weapon under his coat. The four men continued their slow walk north on Fourth Street.

The gang members were waiting near Fly's Photo Gallery. Virgil called out, "Throw up your arms. I have come to disarm you."[3]

Billy and Frank cocked their pistols. Tom jumped behind Frank's horse. In the next instant the firing started. Billy's shot went wild, but Wyatt's slug knocked Frank to the ground. Doc, shotgun at the ready, looked for a target. Ike, who was unarmed, wrestled briefly with Wyatt, then fled for cover. Doc wasted a shot trying to bring down the running man.

Morgan shot Billy twice. Frank's frightened horse bolted, leaving Tom exposed. Doc leveled the shotgun and blasted him with the second barrel. Then he drew his pistol.

Despite their wounds, Billy and Frank still had some fight left. Billy plugged Morgan in the shoulder. Frank yelled at Doc, "I've got you this time!"

"You're a good one if you have," Doc snapped back.[4]

Town wits liked to joke that Doc was so thin he vanished when he turned sideways. Frank's next shot proved them wrong. His bullet sliced through Doc's holster and tore a groove across his back. Doc fired back, hitting Frank in the heart.

Billy, slumped against the wall, put a bullet in Virgil's leg. "Give me some more cartridges," he gasped as he tried to lift his empty pistol.[5]

The gunfight was over as quickly as it had started. Both McLaurys were dead. Billy was dying. Doc, Virgil, and Morgan were all wounded. As Doc limped off to find a doctor, he carried a growing legend. He had been raised to be a southern gentleman. History remembers him as a cold-blooded cardsharp and gunslinger.

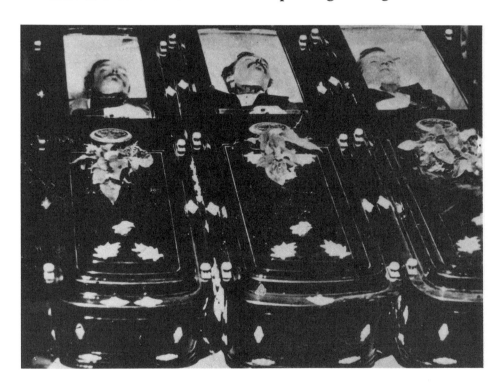

When the smoke cleared after the shootout, three members of the Clanton gang lay dead and dying. After the undertakers did their work, the townsfolk came by to take a last look at (left to right) Tom McLaury, Frank McLaury, and Billy Clanton.

2

A GEORGIA CHILDHOOD

The baby who grew up to be Doc Holliday was born early in 1852 in Griffin, Georgia. No birth record exists, but John Henry Holliday was baptized on March 21. The baby's parents, Henry and Alice McKey Holliday, were greatly respected in the small town. They owned over forty pieces of land. In those pre-Civil War days they also owned six slaves.

Blond blue-eyed John was an only child. An older sister died before he was born.[1] The boy was not lonely, for Henry and Alice helped raise numerous nieces and nephews. John was very close to his gentle, beautiful mother. His relations with his stern father were less tender. Any misstep, large or small, brought swift punishment.

Griffin's peaceful life ended early in January 1861. Georgia left the Union and joined the Confederate States

Doc Holliday seldom posed for the camera. This photo is one of the few that have been accepted as authentic portraits of the Wild West's most famous dentist.

of America. In April the first shots of the Civil War rang out at Fort Sumter, South Carolina. A loyal Southerner, Henry joined the Confederate army. As a veteran of the Mexican War, he was given the rank of captain. A few weeks later his regiment marched off to fight in Virginia.

The North set up a naval blockade that brought hardships to the home folk. Soap, shoes, thread, tea, pins, and other factory goods grew scarce. Letters from soldiers at the front told of even greater hardships.

By July 1862 a third of Henry's regiment lay dead or wounded. Henry escaped the bullets, only to fall ill. He resigned from the army and returned home, sick and nearly broke. As the Confederate dollar collapsed, so did his fortunes. To start over, he moved his family south to Valdosta. The raw half-built Georgia town lay at the edge of the wilderness.

Ten-year-old John jumped headlong into his new life. When he was away from his father's stern gaze he was a happy, mischievous child. He loved to ride, shoot, and fish. On lazy summer days he swam with his friends in the Withlacoochee River. Because Valdosta lacked a public school, the Hollidays helped start a private school. John struggled to master Greek, Latin, and French as well as the three 'R's.

In September 1864 the Union army marched across

Young John Holliday grew up in the turmoil of the Civil War and its aftermath. In this engraving, the artist captured a busy postwar scene. Ex-slaves, army veterans, shopkeepers, and frontiersmen share an unpaved street with pigs, horses, and cattle.

Georgia. Atlanta fell. After burning this city, General William T. Sherman led his troops on a march to the sea. Yankee looters set fire to all that lay in their path. Food grew scarce. The Hollidays lived on the turnips, beets, and collard greens that they grew in their garden.

The long savage war ended in April 1865. Carpetbaggers and scalawags took over Valdosta, as they did elsewhere in the South. At the Holliday house Henry struggled to keep a tight rein on his son. John hated the politicians who grew fat while his friends and family went hungry.

In 1866 John finished his schooling. The slim, wiry teenager had shot up to 5 feet 10 inches. In those days a fourteen-year-old was almost an adult. The family talked about sending him to college to study law. Then, on September 16, John's mother died of tuberculosis. Henry added to his son's grief when he remarried a year later. John refused to accept young Rachel Holliday as his new mother. His only joy came from courting his cousin Mattie. John hoped to marry the great love of his life, but the families refused. Mattie, who was Catholic, later entered a convent.[2]

Four years later John suddenly left town. The reason is far from clear. One legend says he was part of a failed plot to blow up the Valdosta courthouse. The only fact not in dispute is that Henry put John on a train leaving Valdosta.

3

PULLING TEETH

In 1870 the age of the village toothpuller was ending. Schools were opening that promised to teach dentistry in a matter of months. When John Holliday left home, he planned to become a dentist. His strong, sure hands seemed well suited to the task.

No one knows how and where John learned his trade. Most western historians believe he went to dental school in Baltimore, Maryland. This city did have a fine dental college. Neither school nor city records, however, list a John Holliday.[1]

If not Baltimore—where? One guess is that John did not go to dental school at all. In those days, a young man could learn dentistry by working as an apprentice. An established dentist might have taken John under his wing. Under the older man's watchful eye, John would have learned to fill and pull teeth. In time he would have

At eighteen, John left home to learn dentistry. In less than a year he learned to pull teeth, make dentures, and fill cavities. Dentists of the period kept the tools of their profession in cabinets like this one.

progressed to making crowns and fitting dentures. He would have used a foot-powered drill and filled cavities with gold foil. Patients paid fifty cents for a filling. A whiff of nitrous oxide might help deaden the pain. A full set of false teeth made of hard rubber cost just $15 in those days.

His dental training finished, John returned to a warm family welcome. Henry soon saw that the news was not all good. Young Doctor Holliday was in ill health. His thin body was wracked by a troubling cough. He felt tired and feverish, and his nerves were on edge. To a medical doctor the signs would have been clear. John's symptoms pointed to the early stages of tuberculosis.

For a time John worked with a dentist in Griffin. When his health did not improve, he moved to Atlanta. The guidebooks had promised a healthy climate. To a young man fresh from small town life, however, it was the nightlife that was exciting. After a day's work, John could go to the theater or look for a game of cards. If his stomach felt upset, he could drink from a free mineral spring. More often he quenched his thirst with beer and whiskey.

John worked in the dental office of Dr. Arthur Ford.[2]

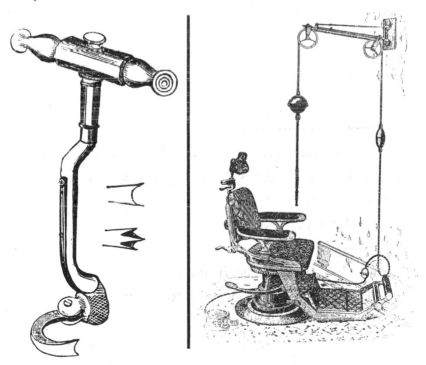

In the mid-1800s, dentistry was gaining acceptance as one of the healing arts. Up-to-date offices featured reclining chairs and foot-powered drills (right). When called on to pull a tooth, the dentist would have picked up a dental key (left).

His constant cough must have alarmed his patients. He lost weight, and most nights woke up soaked with sweat. Morning meant a wretched spell of coughing and spitting. When he began to cough up blood, he finally went to see a doctor.

The doctor confirmed John's worst fears. He had tuberculosis. Some writers think he caught the disease from his mother. Others suggest his patients may have infected him.[3]

This is a disease without a cure, the doctor said. Stay in Georgia, and you will be dead within six months. The only hope, he added, is to move to a high, dry climate. The doctor believed that out west, in Texas or Colorado, John might add a year or two to his life span.[4]

Grimly, John set about putting his life in order. He no longer dreamed of marrying Mattie. In a letter to his father he outlined his dilemma. Henry met him in Atlanta and helped John plan what future he had left. To raise money they sold some land John's mother had left him.

In November 1872, father and son said goodbye. John looked much older than his twenty-one years as he boarded the westbound train. Ahead lay a new life in Dallas, Texas.

4

ENTER DOC HOLLIDAY

In 1872 the route to Dallas was neither direct nor quick. John traveled by train, riverboat, and coastal steamer as far as Galveston. From there a Texas Central train hauled him the final bumpy miles.

If John needed a high, dry climate, he did not find it in Dallas. Still, the booming frontier town pleased him. Cowboys making the long trek to Kansas drove longhorn cattle through the streets. Retail stores and saloons did a roaring business. In Atlanta, John had risked arrest by playing a hand of poker. Here a man with money never lacked for a game, a drink, or a woman.

A local dentist, Dr. John A. Seegar, took the soft-spoken Georgian into his office. Seegar, twenty years older, was well respected in Dallas. Records show that John's father sold a second property in March 1873.

17

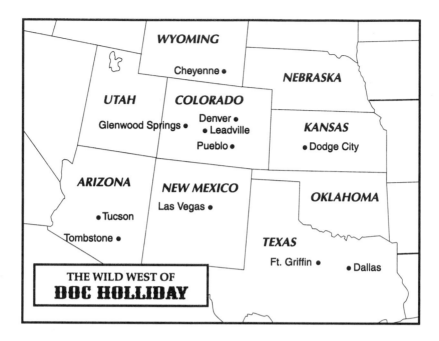

After leaving Georgia, Doc Holliday moved west, looking for a healthy climate. His restless nature took him to some of the toughest towns in the Wild West.

The money most likely paid John's way into practice with Seegar. The two shared an office on Elm Street, between Market and Austin.

Young Dr. Holliday dressed well and spoke with a southern accent. He kept his blond mustache well trimmed. Even so, his waiting room was often empty. Whatever his skills with a tooth extractor, his coughing must have driven patients away. As time went on he spent less time at the office—and more time with the bottle.

John had started drinking in Atlanta. He thought that liquor helped him cope with troubled, sleepless nights. As Wyatt Earp later remarked, "Two and three

18

quarts of liquor a day was not unusual for him, yet I never saw him stagger. . . . At times . . . it would take a pint of whiskey to get him going in the morning."[1]

The bottle was not John's only friend. His quick mind and deft hands made him a natural at the gaming tables. Playing cards kept away morbid thoughts of death. Gambling at faro also put money in his pocket. The saloon crowd called him "Doc" Holliday, the gambling dentist.

In a faro game, the dealer turns up two cards at a time from a wooden box. Players bet on which of the thirteen cards, ace to king, would turn up. The first card was a loser; the second card was a winner. Some decks had a tiger printed on the ace of spades. Faro players, therefore, were said to be "bucking the tiger."

In a frontier saloon, fights were nightly affairs. With his bitter sneering tongue, Doc started more than his share. The thin, sickly dentist did not dare fight with his fists. Bat Masterson put it this way: "Doc Holliday was a weakling who could not have whipped a healthy fifteen-year-old boy in a go-as-you-please fist fight."[2]

To even the odds, Doc carried a cut down Colt .45. The short barrel made it easy to hide. Weeks of practice helped him develop a lightning draw. His shooting was another matter. The record shows that he missed his target more often than not. One reason was that the Colt kicked like a mule. Doc was not strong enough to hold the gun steady.

Three years slipped by. Doc took pride in having proven the Atlanta doctor wrong. Given only a year to live, he was still alive and kicking. That state of affairs almost changed on New Year's Day in 1875.

Doc was playing cards with a saloonkeeper named Charles Austin. One hard word led to many more. All at once each man went for his gun. Both fired—and both missed. The shooters were then locked up for disturbing the peace.[3]

The gunplay alarmed the town's more peaceful citizens. Doc was asked to leave. When he pulled out, his days as a dentist were mostly behind him.

Doc's passion for gambling grew as his dental practice declined. When he sat down at the faro table, no one paid much attention to his constant coughing. It was at crowded tables like this that he won fame as a gambler and quick-on-the-trigger gunfighter.

5

FOOTLOOSE ON THE FRONTIER

Doc Holliday was twenty-three when he left Dallas in the spring of 1875. A legend was growing around him. Did he really shoot a patient who complained too loudly? No record of the shooting exists, but the story refuses to die.[1]

Doc had heard that Fort Griffin, Texas—150 miles to the west—was "hell-on-the-border."[2] After leaving Dallas he went to see for himself. He found a wide-open frontier outpost on the cattle trail that led north to Dodge City, Kansas. Buffalo hunters camped nearby. The stench of rotting hides warned newcomers that they were nearing Fort Griffin.

Saloons and gambling halls lined the town's main street. Hunters, cowboys, and soldiers came to town eager to spend their pay. Doc did his best to help them do so.

Faro was only one of Doc's games. If the action at the card tables was slow, he could move to the craps tables. This saloon guaranteed that its dice were square, but Doc kept a wary eye open for cheaters. Hard experience had taught him all the tricks of the gambler's trade.

As an actor practices his lines, Doc rehearsed his card skills. He learned flashy shuffles, cuts, and other useful tricks. His nimble fingers could make a false cut that left a stacked deck unchanged. When he needed an edge, he sometimes dealt from the bottom of the deck. A better trick was dealing "seconds"—leaving the top card and dealing the next. Because he knew all the tricks, he was good at spotting cheaters.

Doc's stay in Fort Griffin later became part of his legend. One story says that he fell head-over-heels in love while he was there. The woman was a red-haired gambler named Lottie Deno. Another story charges Doc with shooting three soldiers, one of whom died.[3]

22

Perhaps Doc did fall in love with the beautiful Lottie. If so, nothing came of it. As for the shooting, no one can prove it happened.

In the midst of Doc's good times, Fort Griffin's sheriff launched a clean-up drive. Faro and poker were illegal, he said, pointing to a seldom-enforced Texas law. In June, Doc was picked up and thrown in jail. Annoyed, he made bail and left town. It seemed foolish to wait around for a trial.

After leaving Texas, Doc traveled by train and stagecoach to Denver, Colorado. He tried to leave the

Doc paid his first visit to Denver in 1875. He very likely stepped off the stagecoach at the Overland Dispatch office (far right in this 1866 engraving). Denver's mountain air eased his breathing, and its faro tables rewarded his skill with cards.

past behind by taking his mother's maiden name. The clean mountain air helped "Tom McKey" breathe more easily. Thanks to his skill as a faro dealer, he was soon making ten dollars a day. With meals a quarter each and hotel rooms a dollar a night, ten dollars was good pay. Because of Denver's gun law, Doc had to leave his pistol in his room. In its place, he hung a knife around his neck.

Early in 1876, gold strikes in the Black Hills of South Dakota grabbed the headlines. Doc went to Cheyenne, Wyoming, to be closer to the action. There he dealt faro and listened to tales of Indian fighting. In June news arrived of General Custer's defeat at the Little Bighorn. Two months later, bad news arrived from the remote gold-mining camp of Deadwood. A gunman had shot

The lure of gold strikes in the Black Hills drew Doc to Cheyenne in 1876. With his ailing lungs, Doc could not go prospecting. He stayed in town and "mined the miners." When he tired of gambling, he sometimes took part in a gold brick swindle.

the famous lawman Wild Bill Hickok in the back of the head. Doc was shaken by Wild Bill's death. From that time on, he sat with his back to the wall when he played cards.

In 1877 Doc played a role in a gold brick swindle. While traveling by train, Doc let his seatmate know that he was a mine owner. Alas, he would confide, the mine was deep in debt. Sadly, he was being forced to sell his last "gold" brick. Dazzled by visions of quick profits, the victim would offer to buy the brick. Doc would strike a deal, grab the money, and vanish. Soon two "detectives" would appear to seize the gilded lead brick "for evidence." Later, the three con men would meet to split the take.[4]

Hard times hit Denver in 1878. When Doc heard that Dodge City was booming, he packed up and headed east to Kansas. He left the name Tom McKey behind, along with a new story to add to his legend. This one says that Doc fled after carving up a gambler named Bud Ryan. Doc did have a hair-trigger temper to be sure. He was capable of knifing someone, but this time he was innocent.[5]

6

DOC MAKES NEW FRIENDS

Dodge City's growth spurt began in 1875. That was the year the first big herds of Texas cattle came up the Chisholm and Western Trails. When Doc stepped off the train in 1878, twelve hundred people lived there. The residents had mixed feelings about the cattle drives. The cowboys who herded the longhorns spent money freely. Mixing high spirits and rotgut whiskey, however, often led to wild gunplay.

Dodge City's police force did its best to keep the peace. A well-dressed dandy named Bat Masterson was sheriff. His brother Ed served as city marshal. It was no job for a man who craved a long and quiet life. Ed was gunned down by a whiskey-crazed cowpoke soon after Doc arrived.

Doc rented Room 24 of the two-story Dodge House. On June 8, 1878, he ran an ad in the Dodge City *Times* that offered dental services. No one knows how much business it drew. His work in Room 24 did give birth to another unconfirmed story. In this one a rival gambler asks to have a tooth filled. Doc knocks the man out with gas—and then pulls all his teeth.

If Doc's coughing did not discourage patients, his temper surely would have. Sober, he often turned the mildest joke into a deadly insult. Before a bewildered stranger could blink, he would be facing a gunfight. Doc took a sour pleasure in seeing his victims cringe and beg off.[1]

Few people saw Doc cold sober. After each morning's coughing spell he downed a bottle of whiskey. The liquor seemed to soothe his tortured spirit. After a late breakfast he would go looking for action. Most days he could find a game at the Long Branch Saloon. That was where he most likely met Kate Elder and Wyatt Earp.

Kate was better known as Big-Nosed Kate. Next to her robust frame, Doc looked smaller and frailer than ever. No one ever accused Kate of being a lady. She was loud, crude, and shared Doc's passion for strong drink. The two made a most unlikely pair.

Legend says that Kate once saved Doc's life. In the hard-to-prove story, both were living in Fort Griffin. A fight broke out over a card game, and Doc killed a man with his bowie knife. Lacking a jail, the sheriff locked Doc in his hotel room. That night, the dead man's friends turned the saloon crowd into a lynch mob. Kate, thinking fast, set fire to a wooden shack. While the town was fighting the fire, she helped Doc escape.[2]

Doc met Wyatt Earp soon after he reached Dodge City. The famous lawman soon became Doc's only real friend. To be sure, the friendship was a strange one. Wyatt upheld law and order; Doc lived on the shady side of the law. Wyatt, cool and sure of himself, tried to avoid gunplay. Doc was hot-headed and quick on the trigger. Wyatt did admire Doc's courage. He also owed Doc his life.

Wyatt described the rescue in an 1886 article. "It wasn't long after I returned to Dodge City that [Doc Holliday's] quickness saved my life," he wrote. "He saw a man draw on me behind my back. 'Look out, Wyatt!' he shouted. While the words were coming out of his mouth he . . . shot the other fellow before [he] could fire."[3]

Kate and Doc moved into a one-room house with a

Dodge City reigned as the queen of the cattle towns. Here, cowboys drive their longhorn cattle through the streets, marking the end of the long trail from Texas.

Wyatt Earp and Doc Holliday were sometimes on opposite sides of the law, but they became lifelong friends. In this photo, Wyatt (bottom row, second from left) posed with his fellow lawmen on the Dodge City Peace Commission.

lean-to kitchen. When the cards were falling his way, Doc bought fancy dresses for Kate. When his luck was bad, he cursed her for being a cheap floozy. They argued, fought, and made up—over and over.[4]

Dodge City was quiet after the herds were shipped off for slaughter. The next two years were quiet, too. Fewer cattle were coming up from Texas. In 1880, Bat and Wyatt went off to try their luck in Tombstone, Arizona. After a good run at the tables, Doc decided to follow his friends.

7
FROM LAS VEGAS TO TOMBSTONE

With Kate at his side, Doc boarded a train and waved goodbye to Dodge City. Although he was on his way to Tombstone, he did not hurry. He and Kate stopped off in Las Vegas, New Mexico.

Doc knew the wild frontier town well. Tiring of Dodge City, he had set up a dental practice there the previous year. As usual, poker paid better than his dental patients did. After building up a stake, he bought into a Central Street saloon.[1] Doc might have settled down for a while, but for Mike Gordon.

Gordon, a former Army scout, had fallen in love with a saloon girl. He had begged the woman to run off with him, but she refused. On June 19, Gordon went a little crazy. He stood in the street and fired a shot into the saloon. When his lady love did not appear, he fired a second wild shot. Doc guessed the next bullet might hit

Legend says that Big-Nosed Kate Fisher (real name, Kate Elder) once saved Doc's life. Whatever the truth of the story, the robust saloon girl loved her alcoholic dentist. Kate followed her man as far as Tombstone before Doc kicked her out for good.

someone. He stepped outside and leveled his pistol. For once, his aim was true. Gordon fell, bleeding from a fatal wound. Fearing arrest, Doc saddled up and returned to Dodge.[2]

When Doc returned to Las Vegas a year later, the shooting was old news. Even so, trouble had a way of finding him. Kate had scarcely unpacked their bags when word reached their hotel. An old enemy named Charlie White was working in a Las Vegas saloon. A few years back Doc had bluffed Charlie into leaving Dodge City. It was time, Doc decided, to finish the job.

Doc stalked into the saloon, gun in hand. As soon as he spotted Charlie he opened fire. The shots went wild. Charlie dived behind the bar as startled patrons ducked for cover. When Charlie appeared again he had a pistol

31

in his hand. The two men blazed away at close range, but neither one hit the other. The shooting ended when Charlie backed into a bullet and crumpled to the floor. Doc turned on his heel and left the saloon. Moments later the "dead man" stood up. The slug had only grazed his spine. Happy to be alive, Charlie did not press his luck. He left town on a train headed east.

Doc walked back to his hotel room. He looked at Kate, smiled, and said, "Got him." Then he reached for a bottle.[3]

It took two quarts of 100-proof whiskey to get Doc through each day. Until he took his first morning drink, his heart fluttered and his hands shook. At twenty-eight, he was a hopeless alcoholic. Hard living and hard drinking had left their marks. His blond hair was graying and his face was gaunt. Fate had stacked the deck against him, but he played the cards he was dealt.

From Las Vegas, Doc moved to Tombstone, the town "too tough to die." Despite the 4,500-foot altitude, the desert heat hit 120° that summer. Dust filled the air, making it hard for Doc to breathe. When it rained the dust turned to rivers of mud. Doc and Kate settled into a house at Allen and Sixth Streets. The one-story adobe was flanked by a funeral parlor and a wine shop.

Four of the Earp brothers had reached Tombstone ahead of him. James, the oldest, made his living as a faro dealer. Virgil, a career lawman, was working his way up to city marshal. Wyatt wore the star of deputy U.S.

Marshal for Pima County. Morgan rode shotgun on the Wells Fargo stages. None were happy to see Doc Holliday.

Doc, the rumors said, had turned stage and train robber. He was supposed to have held up the Santa Fe-Las Vegas stage twice in August 1879. Two months later, it was said, he had robbed a train.[4] These stories put Wyatt in a bind. Doc was his friend, but a peace officer was sworn to uphold the law. In the end friendship won. After all, if a fight broke out, Doc was a good man to have on your side.

Tombstone's elegant Birdcage Theater gave fun-starved miners a good run for their money. After watching the lively stage show, the men could drink, gamble, and dance as long as their money held out. Doc and other gamblers tried to make sure they left with empty pockets.

8
A TROUBLED TIME IN TOMBSTONE

Tombstone owed much of its lawlessness to the Clanton gang. Old Man Clanton and his sons owned a ranch near town. Their gang, known as the Cowboys, robbed stages and rustled cattle. Sheriff John Behan could be counted on to turn a blind eye to their crimes.

Doc felt at home in the shabby mining town. He spent his working hours at the card tables. When Wyatt needed backup, he was there to help.

A loudmouth named Johnny Tyler gave Doc a chance to show his stuff. Tyler and his rowdy friends were keeping the Oriental Saloon in an uproar. They drove customers away by starting fights and cursing at the dealers. When the owner asked Wyatt for help, the lawman grabbed Tyler's ear and dragged him outside. Doc, bringing up the rear, kept Tyler's buddies from shooting his friend in the back.

Tyler ran to retrieve his gun. When he returned to the saloon, he challenged Doc to step outside. "What's wrong with where we stand?" Doc said with a sneer. "Ready?" The look in Doc's eyes told Tyler this was not a bluff. He turned and ran. Doc strolled to the door and watched him go. "[He's] still running," he observed. Within a few days Tyler was laughed out of town.[1]

In March 1881 bandits botched a holdup of the Tucson stage. After the driver was killed, the frightened horses bolted. A plucky guard regained control of the runaways and drove the stage to safety. As the town buzzed with the news, the Clantons saw a chance to discredit the Earps. They accused Doc of taking part in the holdup. Doc felt he had been insulted. "If I'd pulled

This panoramic view was once labeled, "A Buzzard's Eye View of Tombstone, Arizona, 1880." Here, the town looks peaceful enough. It was only a year later that Doc and the Earps took the long walk that ended in the Shootout at the O.K. Corral.

Until the railroads came, the Wild West relied on stagecoaches to carry passengers and mail. There were no soldiers riding shotgun the day that bandits tried to hold up the Tucson stage. Doc was accused of taking part in the holdup. For once, his protests of innocence were probably true.

that job, I'd have gotten the eighty thousand," he told the saloon crowd.[2]

Sheriff Behan, prodded by the Clantons, was looking for a reason to arrest Doc. He found it when Doc and Kate had a furniture-smashing fight. After Doc moved out, Behan treated the tearful Kate to a bottle of gin. When she was drunk he gave her a paper to sign. In the paper she swore that Doc had admitted to holding up the stage. The next day, sober and repentant, Kate withdrew her statement. With no real proof against Doc, the case was thrown out of court.

Kate's change of heart came too late. Doc's love had turned to loathing. When they met he cursed her. Kate cursed him back, talked him out of a chunk of cash, and left town.

Meanwhile, Wyatt had been dealing with Ike Clanton. In return for the $3,600 reward, Ike agreed to lead the stage robbers into a trap. Before the trap could be sprung, all three died in shootouts in New Mexico. That left Ike with a new worry. What if the Cowboys learned of the double cross he had planned? The Earps—and Doc—had to be silenced.

Ike drank too much on the night of October 25. As he lurched around town he bragged that the Cowboys were going to do some killing. Doc caught up with him in a lunchroom. "I hear you're going to kill me," Doc snarled. "Get out your gun and commence."[3]

Ike held up his hands to show he was not armed. Doc ordered Ike to carry a gun if he was going to shoot off his mouth. Their standoff set the scene for the gunfight at the O.K. Corral.

The bloody October shootout did not end the violence. In December, firing from ambush, someone shattered Virgil's arm with a shotgun blast. Three months later, three gunmen shot Morgan in the back.

The names of the Clanton men who had killed Morgan soon surfaced. Wyatt and Doc went on the warpath. They followed Frank Stilwell to Tucson, where they left his bullet-riddled body beside the railroad tracks. A day later they caught up with Florentino Cruz. They shot him, too. Then, with murder charges hanging over their heads, Doc and Wyatt fled to Colorado.

9
A LEGEND DIES
WITH HIS BOOTS OFF

Doc and Wyatt split up when they reached Colorado. Doc was worn out by his two years in Tombstone. He stayed in Pueblo while Wyatt went on to try his luck in Gunnison. The two friends never met again.

Two months later Doc paid a visit to Denver. There he ran into a bounty hunter named Perry Mallan. Mallan arrested Doc and asked to have him sent to Arizona for trial. Bat Masterson used his influence with the governor to stop the extradition. Governor Pitkin agreed that Doc would not receive a fair trial in Tombstone.[1]

In 1883 Doc moved to the booming mining town of Leadville. At first the 10,200-foot altitude left him gasping for breath. He collapsed when he tried to walk down the street. When he adjusted to the thin air, he

After leaving Tombstone, Doc tried his luck in Colorado. He stopped briefly in Denver, then moved on to the bustling mining town of Leadville. Trouble and bad health dogged his footsteps. After a shooting scrape, Doc moved back to Denver.

Doc checked himself into the Glenwood Springs health spa in 1887. The years of hard living, combined with tuberculosis, had turned him into a gray-haired old man. Defiant to the end, Doc's last act on earth was to call for his boots and a drink of whiskey.

took a job dealing faro at the Monarch Saloon. The owner hoped Doc's fame would attract customers.

Pneumonia put Doc in bed for a few weeks. When he returned to work, Johnny Tyler was waiting. Doc's old foe from Tombstone then sent a friend to pick a fight. Doc caused a nasty scene and lost his job. Too sick to work, he ran short of money.

Doc pawned his watch, but not his gun. On August 19, 1884, Billy Allen found Doc in a saloon and rushed at him, fists raised. Allen was angry because Doc owed him five dollars. Outweighed by seventy pounds, Doc did the sensible thing: he drew his gun. Allen stumbled as he tried to retreat and Doc shot him in the arm. It was Doc's last gunfight. He was charged with attempted murder, but a friendly jury set him free.[2]

Back in Denver, Doc's luck went from bad to worse. In August 1886 he was jailed for running up debts that he could not pay. A year later he moved to

40

Glenwood Springs. Breathing the health resort's sulphur fumes hastened the collapse of his lungs. By September he was confined to his bed. Dreams of death haunted his sleep.

On the morning of November 8, Doc woke with a clear head. He asked for a drink of whiskey and begged the nurse to fetch his boots. His request came too late. Doc died as he had feared he might, with his boots off.[3]

Doctor John Holliday was already a legend when he was buried at age thirty-five. Everyone "knew" that Doc had killed dozens of men. The real number, it turns out, is closer to four or five. Stories of Doc's dead-eye shooting are also mostly fiction. The record shows that he missed his targets more often than he hit them.

Did this soft-spoken, mean-tempered alcoholic have a good side? His friends praised his courage and his loyalty. He stood by Wyatt Earp when he could easily have gone his own way. Mattie Holliday loved him, as did Kate Elder. Bat Masterson did not like him, but blamed his angry nature on too much whiskey.

Doc's lawyer once asked his client if his conscience bothered him. "No," Doc replied. "I coughed that up with my lungs long ago."[4] John "Doc" Holliday was a violent man, but so were the times in which he lived.

NOTES BY CHAPTER

Chapter 1

1. Paula Mitchell Marks, *And Die in the West: The Story of the O.K. Corral Gunfight* (New York: William Morrow and Co., 1989), p. 215.

2. Paul Trachtman and the editors of Time-Life Books, *The Gunfighters* (Alexandria, Va.: Time-Life Books, 1974), p. 27.

3. Pat Jahns, *The Frontier World of Doc Holliday* (New York: Indian Head Books, 1957), p. 210.

4. John Myers, *Doc Holliday* (Boston: Little, Brown and Company, 1955), p. 170.

5. Trachtman, p. 33.

Chapter 2

1. John Myers, *Doc Holliday* (Boston: Little, Brown and Company, 1955), p. 12.

2. Pat Jahns, *The Frontier World of Doc Holliday* (New York: Indian Head Books, 1957), pp. 24–25.

Chapter 3

1. Dale T. Schoenberger, *The Gunfighters* (Caldwell, Idaho: Caxton Printers, Ltd., 1971), p. 94.

2. Howard R. Lamar, *The Reader's Encyclopedia of the American West* (New York: Thomas Crowell, 1977), p. 507.

3. Dan L. Thrapp, *Encyclopedia of Frontier Biography*, Vol. II (Glendale, Calif.: Arthur H. Clark Co., 1988), p. 670.

4. Pat Jahns, *The Frontier World of Doc Holliday* (New York: Indian Head Books, 1957), p. 37.

Chapter 4

1. Quoted in John Myers, *Doc Holliday* (Boston: Little, Brown and Company, 1955), p. 51.

2. W. B. (Bat) Masterson, *Famous Gunfighters of the Western Frontier* (Fort Davis, Tex.: Frontier Book Company, 1968), pp. 35–36.

3. Dale T. Schoenberger, *The Gunfighters* (Caldwell, Idaho: Caxton Printers, Ltd., 1971), p. 96.

Chapter 5

1. Dan L. Thrapp, *Encyclopedia of Frontier Biography*, Vol. II (Glendale, Calif.: Arthur H. Clark Co., 1988), p. 670.

2. Pat Jahns, *The Frontier World of Doc Holliday* (New York: Indian Head Books, 1957), p. 52.

3. Thrapp, p. 670.

4. Jahns, pp. 81–82.

5. Ibid. p. 84.

Chapter 6

1. Jay Robert Nash, *Encyclopedia of World Crime*, Vol. II (Wilmette, Ill.: CrimeBooks, 1990), p. 1,593.

2. Carl Sifakis, *The Encyclopedia of American Crime* (New York: Facts on File, 1982), p. 341.

3. Wyatt Earp, writing in the *San Francisco Examiner* (Sunday, August 2, 1896).

4. Pat Jahns, *The Frontier World of Doc Holliday* (New York: Indian Head Books, 1957), p. 115.

Chapter 7

1. John Myers, *Doc Holliday* (Boston: Little, Brown and Company, 1955), pp. 112–113.

2. Bill O'Neal, *Encyclopedia of Western Gunfighters* (Norman, Okla.: University of Oklahoma Press, 1979), p. 145.

3. Pat Jahns, *The Frontier World of Doc Holliday* (New York: Indian Head Books, 1957), pp. xi, 141.

4. Dan L. Thrapp, *Encyclopedia of Frontier Biography*, Vol. II (Glendale, Calif.: Arthur H. Clark Co., 1988), p. 670.

Chapter 8

1. Pat Jahns, *The Frontier World of Doc Holliday* (New York: Indian Head Books, 1957), pp. 153–154.

2. Jay Robert Nash, *Encyclopedia of World Crime*, Vol. II (Wilmette, Ill.: CrimeBooks, 1990), p. 1,594.

3. John Myers, *Doc Holliday* (Boston: Little, Brown and Company, 1955), p. 159.

Chapter 9

1. Howard R. Lamar, *The Reader's Encyclopedia of the American West* (New York: Thomas Crowell, 1977), p. 508.

2. Bill O'Neal, *Encyclopedia of Western Gunfighters* (Norman, Okla.: University of Oklahoma Press, 1979), p. 146.

3. Jay Robert Nash, *Encyclopedia of World Crime*, Vol. II (Wilmette, Ill.: CrimeBooks, 1990), p. 1,594.

4. Quoted in John Myers, *Doc Holliday* (Boston: Little, Brown and Company, 1955), p. 263.

GLOSSARY

adobe—Sundried bricks made of clay and straw. A building made of these bricks is also called an adobe.

alcoholic—A person who is addicted to alcohol.

bail—Money paid to a court to guarantee the return of a suspect for trial.

bounty hunter—A person who captures or kills fugitives in order to collect a reward.

bowie knife—A hunting knife.

cardsharp—A gambler who cheats at cards.

carpetbaggers—Northern politicians who went to the South after the Civil War to take over state and local governments.

Civil War—The war between the North and the South, 1861–1865.

Confederate—A term used to describe the southern cause during the Civil War.

con man—A slang term for a confidence man. Con men swindle gullible people by preying on their greed.

corral—A fenced area used for keeping horses or cattle.

crown—A gold or enamel covering used by a dentist to repair a broken or decayed tooth.

dentures—The more formal name for false teeth.

dime novels—Popular fiction printed in low-cost books and magazines during the late 1800s.

extradite—To return accused criminals to the state or country in which they will stand trial.

faro—A popular card game in the Wild West. Gamblers bet on their ability to guess the top card of the dealer's pack.

frontier—A region just being opened to settlers.

jury—A group of citizens sworn to judge the facts and give a verdict in a court case.

legend—A story that many people believe, but which is often untrue in whole or in part.

lynch mob—An out-of-control crowd that wants to hang someone.

44

nitrous oxide—A colorless sweet-smelling gas that is used as a dental anesthetic. The popular name for nitrous oxide is laughing gas.

pistol-whipped—Beaten with a pistol.

scalawags—Southern politicians who profited by working with northern carpetbaggers in the years after the Civil War.

tuberculosis—A contagious disease that attacks and destroys the lining of the lungs.

Union—The name given to the northern states that fought against the South during the Civil War.

Yankee—A nickname for Union supporters during and after the Civil War.

MORE GOOD READING
ABOUT DOC HOLLIDAY

DeArment, Robert K. *Bat Masterson: The Man and the Legend*. Norman, Okla.: University of Oklahoma Press, 1979.

Jahns, Pat. *The Frontier World of Doc Holliday*. New York: Indian Head Books, 1957.

Marks, Paula Mitchell. *And Die in the West: The Story of the O.K. Corral Gunfight*. New York: William Morrow and Co., 1989.

Masterson, W. B. (Bat). *Famous Gunfighters of the Western Frontier*. Fort Davis, Tex.: Frontier Book Company, 1968.

Metz, Leon Claire. *The Shooters*. El Paso, Tex.: Mangan Books, 1976.

Myers, John. *Doc Holliday*. Boston: Little, Brown and Company, 1955.

Schoenberger, Dale T. *The Gunfighters*. Caldwell, Idaho: Caxton Printers, Ltd., 1971.

INDEX